Westward EXPANSION

by Cheryl Harness

CONTENTS

Introduction

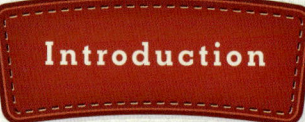

AS THE COLONISTS LOOKED WEST

A young, growing nation viewed the western frontier as a land of hope and promise for the future.

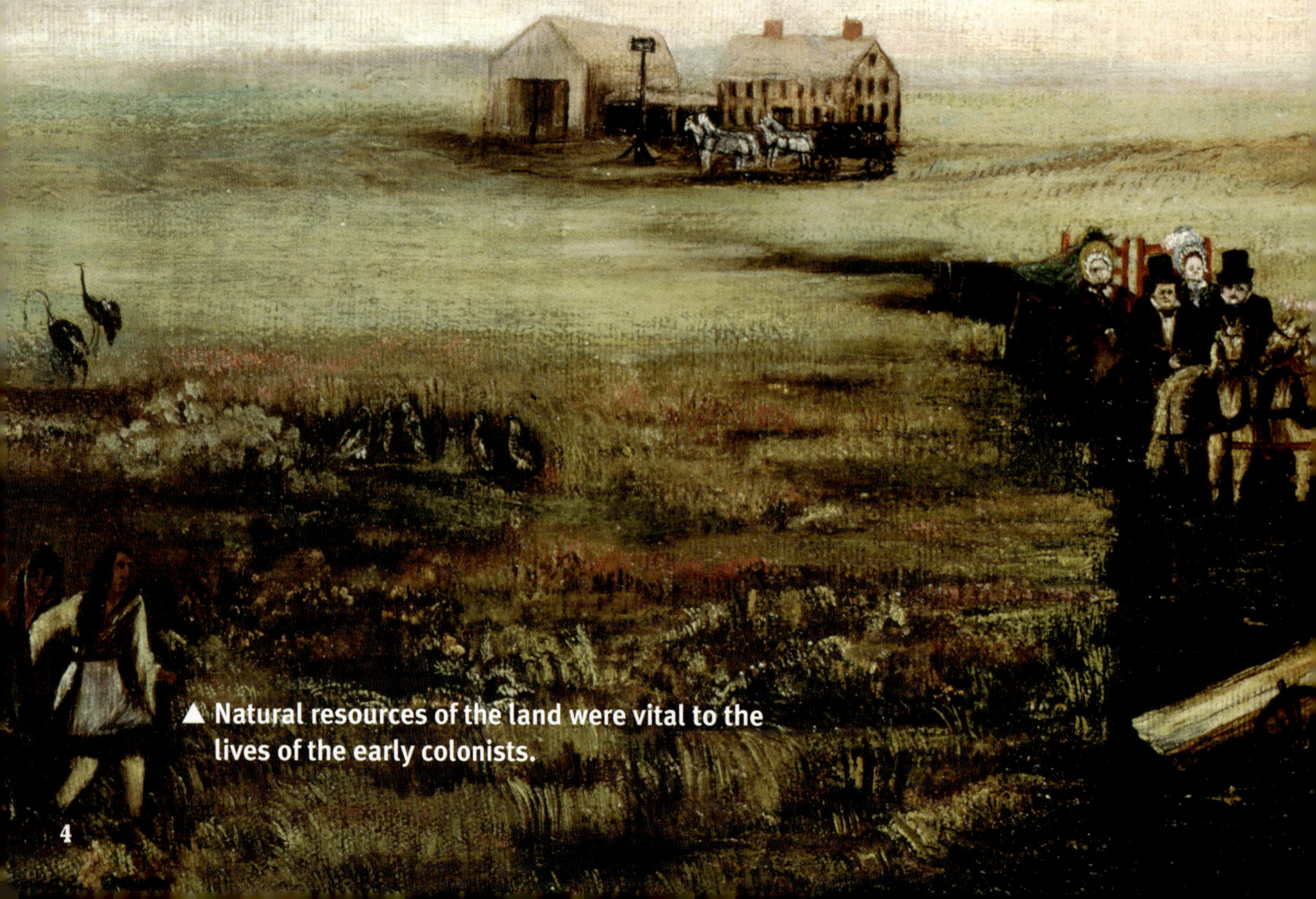

▲ Natural resources of the land were vital to the lives of the early colonists.

In the 1760s, the thirteen British colonies that lined the Atlantic coast were home to as many as 1,600,000 colonists. While a fair number of colonial Americans made their livings as craftspeople and merchants, most of colonial America relied directly on the natural resources of the land and water. They worked each day, hunting, trapping, fishing, farming, and chopping down trees. Felled trees were dragged along logging trails to sawmills. These mills were built on rivers, where fast-moving water wheels turned the saws, transforming the logs into lumber. This lumber was then used to build houses and barns for the growing families and hopeful immigrants who continued to flock to the colonies over the next few decades. In 1790, census-takers counted 3,929,214 people living in the United States. The number had more than doubled since 1763.

As cities grew more crowded and cultivatable land along the eastern seaboard grew scarce, Americans began to look west. As Daniel Boone put it, Americans needed "More elbow room!" To the newly independent nation, the West seemed to promise room enough for everybody.

▲ Early American settlers were eager to explore what lay beyond their western horizon.

VENTURING OUT

Who were the early Americans who pushed westward, and why did they go?

When European explorers sailed west across the Atlantic Ocean and landed on the continent of North America, they were quick to claim vast pieces of land for their royal sponsors back home. Explorers were dazzled by the land's possibilities. Their eagerness to tame it, map it, measure it, and mine its natural resources made them want to keep traveling westward, into the interior.

Early Fur Trappers and Traders

Even before British colonists arrived at Jamestown, Virginia, and Plymouth, Massachusetts, in the early 1600s, the French had begun navigating North America's lakes and rivers. French fur traders exchanged metal pots, weapons, and tools with Native American trappers for fox, otter, bison, and mink **pelts**. Trappers could trade the animal skins and furs for gunpowder, lead, salt, and other things the Native Americans came to desire. From the late 1500s to the mid-1800s, the most valuable pelts of all were the thick, glossy coats of beavers.

Their fur was made into luxurious beaver-felt hats, much desired on both sides of the Atlantic.

The demand for fur led to the development of trading posts along America's lakes and rivers. Some of these posts grew into great cities, such as Detroit, Michigan, and St. Louis, Missouri. Frontiersmen plunged into the woods, splashing through icy streams with their beaver traps. From Native Americans they learned how to make canoes, snowshoes, and long sleds called toboggans, on which they piled their bundles of pelts. These frontiersmen were the first European pioneers, or settlers of the region west of the colonies, and they spearheaded America's expansion. Their knowledge of the wilderness grew as they mapped out trails, found sources of water, and learned to survive the harsh weather. These men would loom large in the story of the American West.

Hats made from beavers' glossy fur were especially prized. ▶

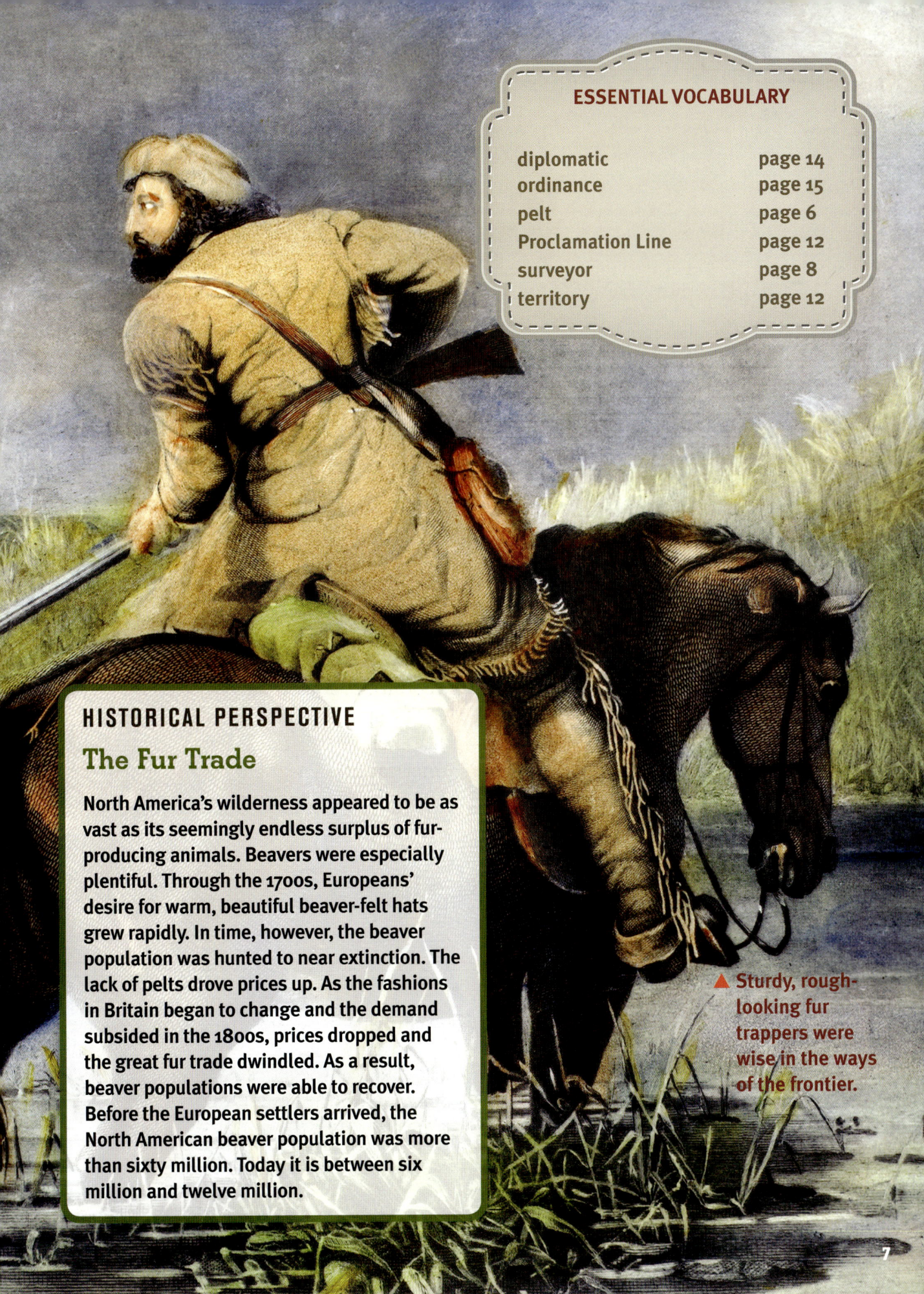

HISTORICAL PERSPECTIVE

The Fur Trade

North America's wilderness appeared to be as vast as its seemingly endless surplus of fur-producing animals. Beavers were especially plentiful. Through the 1700s, Europeans' desire for warm, beautiful beaver-felt hats grew rapidly. In time, however, the beaver population was hunted to near extinction. The lack of pelts drove prices up. As the fashions in Britain began to change and the demand subsided in the 1800s, prices dropped and the great fur trade dwindled. As a result, beaver populations were able to recover. Before the European settlers arrived, the North American beaver population was more than sixty million. Today it is between six million and twelve million.

▲ Sturdy, rough-looking fur trappers were wise in the ways of the frontier.

By the mid-1700s, the fur trade grew so profitable that France and Great Britain began to fight over control of North America and its resources. From 1754 to 1763, the French and Indian War was fought between France and Great Britain on North American soil and elsewhere in the world. The Iroquois Confederacy, a league of Native American groups living in the Northeast region of North America, sided with the British. Most other Native Americans sided with the French. Many Native American tribes had clashed with the fierce Iroquois in the past. They also saw that most of the Europeans settling their lands were from the countries of the British Isles: England, Scotland, Ireland, and Wales. The French, less numerous in North America than the British, cultivated good relations with the Native Americans, while the British settlers often did not.

In the rough country north and west of New York and Pennsylvania, colonists fought alongside the royal, red-coated troops against the French and Native Americans. Among them was young George Washington, who would, decades later, lead the American army against the "redcoats" in the American Revolutionary War.

Measuring the Land

One fundamental difference between the colonists and the Native Americans was how they viewed the land and its resources. To the colonists of North America, the idea of ownership and property was paramount. Owning land meant having the right to hunt and trap its animals, chop down its trees, and build a house, a mill, or a church upon it. As landowners, they could farm the fertile soil or sell it to someone else. So it was important to know exactly who owned what land, and where property borders began and ended.

Surveyors reviewed and measured the land and marked where boundary lines should be drawn on maps or legal documents. Maps showed the shape of a section of land as well as who legally owned or controlled it. In colonial America, at the edge of a vast, unmapped continent, surveying was a very important trade.

HISTORY & LITERATURE

The Pioneers

The Pioneers (1823) is one of many books by James Fenimore Cooper (1789–1851) in which he describes the appearance of his famous character, Natty "Hawkeye" Bumppo, an American frontiersman of the 1700s:

"A kind of coat, made of dressed deer-skin, with the hair on, was belted close to his lank body. . . . On his feet were deer-skin moccasins, ornamented with porcupines' quills . . . and his limbs were guarded with long leggings of the same material. . . . Over his left shoulder was slung a belt of deer-skin, from which [hung] an enormous ox horn, so thinly scraped as to [show] the powder it contained."

The concept of property and ownership was not shared by most Native Americans. For the Native Americans, land was a shared resource, to be used and cared for, not owned or bought or sold. They did not think it was any person's right to own, sell, or purchase this resource. So when tribal leaders signed a treaty, "selling" their lands, they often thought that they were only giving settlers the right to use it, too. As time passed, this misunderstanding led to major conflicts between Native Americans and settlers.

THEY MADE A DIFFERENCE

George Washington: Colonial Surveyor

"The want of accurate Maps of the Country . . . has been a great disadvantage to me." —George Washington's letter to John Hancock, the president of the Continental Congress, January 26, 1777. (Washington was not yet president at the time this letter was written.)

At age 15, in 1747, George Washington started studying surveying. At 17, he was an official surveyor, paid to explore and measure the wilds of colonial Virginia.

His superior math and outdoor skills aided him in his work. He used drafting tools, including a surveyor's compass, or "circumferentor," mounted upon a pole known as a Jacob's staff, or a tripod, to work out a property line's direction. For measuring, he used a 100-link chain, 20 meters (66 feet) long.

United Kingdom
France
Spain

▲ This map marks the division of control over the North American colonies in the mid-1700s.

▼ Before he became a soldier, George Washington worked as a surveyor, measuring the land.

The Settlers

In the 1600s, the colonists lived comparatively close to the frontier. Only about 160 kilometers (100 miles) beyond their coastal settlements was the forested, mountainous backcountry, beyond which lay the largely uncharted interior of the continent. To the colonists, this wilderness held the promise of property ownership, something nearly impossible in Europe. Settling on your own land meant constant hard work, but succeeding meant providing for your family and its future.

The settlers used axes and primitive plows to clear away the trees, stumps, and boulders so they could plant. They built houses for themselves, with heavy logs and stones, and barns for their livestock—namely, chickens, sheep, cattle, pigs, and horses. Often, the settlers joined together in building a stockade or a fort for their protection against invading Native American groups.

Hard work and determination were key to the life of the settlers. ▼

Settlers built fences around their pastures, gardens, and orchards, and planted fields with wheat, corn, barley, tobacco, oats, or flax. They built lumber mills to convert timber to usable building supplies and gristmills, where grain was ground into flour. With sap from maple trees they made syrup and sugar. When men and boys were not working in the fields, they hunted, trapped, and fished. Women and girls spun flax fibers and sheep's wool into thread, which they wove into woolen or linen cloth for their families' clothing and bedding. Food, clothing, and shelter came from the land.

By the early 1700s, European settlers had pushed inland nearly 320 kilometers (200 miles) to the hills and valleys east of the Appalachian Mountains. In time, the settlements became villages and towns. The settlers' children grew up and had families of their own who wanted to settle on their own land. They would travel westward to find it. Immigrants arriving in record numbers also looked to the west for a chance to own property.

Conflicts with the Native Americans

By the mid-1700s, settlers had flooded into the western parts of Pennsylvania, New York, Virginia, and the Carolinas. The impact on the native peoples who populated America at the time of the Europeans' arrival was grave. Sickness, primarily in the form of smallpox, wiped out Native American families and whole tribes in some areas. From the 1600s through the 1800s, countless Native Americans—perhaps as many as 90 percent in some areas—died because they had never been exposed to, and had no immunities against, the diseases brought by the newcomers.

To complicate the situation, Europeans often believed themselves superior to the Native Americans. To Europeans of that era, most Native American groups appeared to be primitive people, with no written language or history. Actually, Native Americans passed their knowledge along in spoken stories and songs. Their spiritual beliefs were different, as well. These cultural misunderstandings made for trouble and, in many cases, deadly violence. Opposing ideas of land ownership led to deadly raids, with Native Americans and European settlers attacking each other's homes and settlements. In the Spanish colonies, thousands of Native Americans were enslaved. Many died of sickness and overwork.

▲ Hostile interactions between European settlers and Native Americans often resulted in loss of life.

HISTORICAL PERSPECTIVE

Pontiac's Rebellion (1763–1766)

Pontiac (c. 1720–1769) was a chief of the Ottawa, a Native American tribe that dwelled in the Ohio Valley. Ottawa warriors helped the French fight the British because a British victory would lead to waves of European settlers pouring into the Native Americans' prime hunting lands along the Ohio River. Because of their victory in the French and Indian War, the British had gained control of almost all of the land between the Atlantic Ocean and the Mississippi River by the spring of 1763. Outraged by the British gains, Pontiac became a great intertribal leader who convinced practically every Indian tribe from Lake Superior to the lower Mississippi to join forces against the British.

▲ Pontiac united various Native American tribes to fight for a common cause.

Pontiac led the tribes in battle and successfully took eight British forts around the Ohio Valley. To keep his hold on the British territories, Pontiac sought the help of his former French allies, but it never came.

In August 1763, in western Pennsylvania, the British defeated Shawnee and Delaware warriors in a key battle. The uprising fell apart, and in time the British reclaimed their forts and Pontiac retreated.

George III was only twenty-two when he became king of Great Britain and Ireland.

The Proclamation Line of 1763

In order to protect the American colonists from continued Native American attack, Great Britain's King George III proclaimed that unless they had a license to trade for furs, settlers, including those who had been in the **territory**, or land, prior to 1763, were not permitted west of an invisible **Proclamation Line**, or border, drawn through the Appalachian Mountains. Beyond the line were the Great Lakes and the Native Americans' hunting lands in the vast valley of the Ohio River. There were also forts where British soldiers were stationed to keep the peace. Many colonial veterans—including George Washington—who had been promised western lands if they helped to defeat the French, were unhappy with the king's decision. In the years to come, smoke from settlers' chimneys drifted over the valleys west of the Appalachian Mountains. For ages, men and women of the Shawnee, Delaware, and other tribes had hunted in woods and meadows there. Now came a trickle of adventurous European hunters.

▼ American colonists faced pressure from their native neighbors as well as their British rulers.

Political Unrest

By 1774, Americans' relationship with their distant British government had grown so difficult that colonial delegates were making their way to the new Continental Congress, in Philadelphia, to decide what to do. An army of colonial militiamen was fighting native warriors throughout the backcountry and helping settlers defend themselves. Late that year, in western Virginia, the colonial soldiers managed to defeat an army of nearly a thousand fighters from the Shawnee, Delaware, and other tribes. The Americans' victory loosened the Native Americans' control over the lands south of the Ohio River, but conflicts between European settlers and the Native Americans would continue during the American Revolution. Throughout the last decades of the 1700s, Native American warriors raided colonial settlements in the Appalachian Mountains, and in the hills and valleys on both sides of the Ohio River.

In April 1775, in Massachusetts, the first shots were fired in America's long war for independence from Great Britain.

✔ **CHECKPOINT**

Read More About It

Read more about eastern Native American tribes, such as the Iroquois, Shawnee, Cherokee, Ottawa, and Seminole, online or in your school library. Compare and contrast how the various tribes lived in the 1700s.

The Old Northwest

The Revolutionary War came to an end with the Treaty of Paris, in 1783. The peace treaty was signed, and an independent United States of America was recognized by the British. Frontier life would continue to be difficult, but Americans took pride in knowing that they were settling a free nation of their own.

According to mutually beneficial **diplomatic** agreements with Great Britain, the United States now had charge of a broad frontier that stretched from the Great Lakes in the north, south to the Ohio River, to Pennsylvania in the east, and west to the Mississippi River. Soon, government-ordered surveyors were on their way to these lands to measure them properly so that sections could be sold to people eager to settle in what would be known as the "Old Northwest."

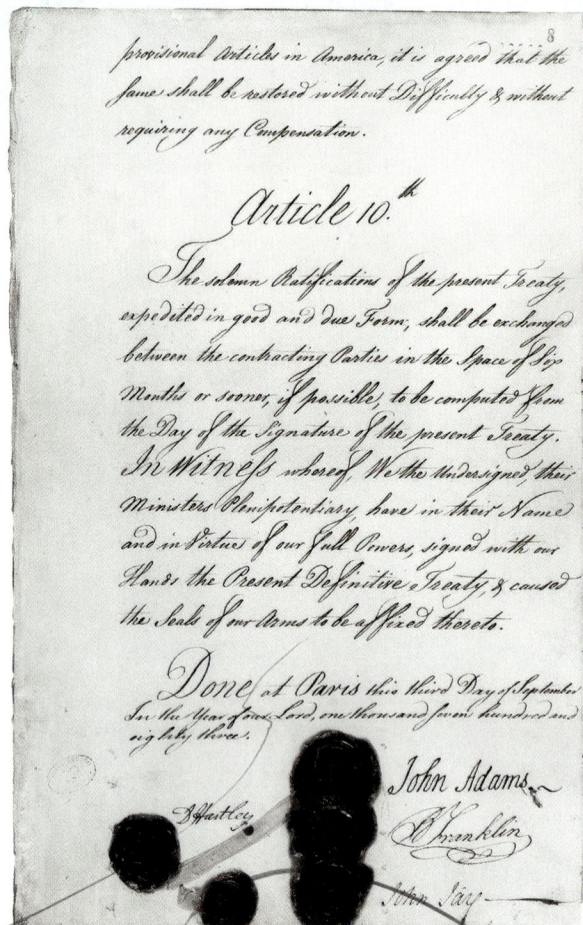

▲ The Treaty of Paris was signed by some of the most important people in American history, such as John Adams, Benjamin Franklin, and John Jay.

THEY MADE A DIFFERENCE

Daniel Boone

Daniel Boone (1723–1820) was a wilderness-wise trailblazer who became one of the first European men to go west into Kentucky. His team of woodsmen cleared what came to be known as Wilderness Road in 1775. They carved and marked this path from the Cumberland Gap to the Kentucky River, where Boone established the settlement of Boonesborough. Wilderness Road was steep and rough, and could be crossed only by foot or by horseback. Thousands of settlers descending upon the region would use the Wilderness Road blazed by Daniel Boone and his team of woodsmen.

The Northwest Ordinance of 1787

The Congress passed the **Ordinance** (or law) of 1785 to see that the Old Northwest was cut into townships that were more than 9.6 kilometers (6 miles) square. Each township would be subdivided into thirty-six equal square sections. Congress reserved sections in every township for the future use of the American government, and it also set aside one section (section 16) in every township for education.

In the Northwest Ordinance of 1787, the lawmakers spelled out how new western lands were to be governed— as official U.S. territories. (The Old Northwest became the Northwest Territory.) When as many as 60,000 people lived in part of the territory, they could apply for statehood. Out of the Northwest Territory came the states of Ohio, Indiana, Illinois, Michigan, Wisconsin, and part of Minnesota.

✔
CHECKPOINT
Make Connections

In 1682 the French explorer René-Robert Cavelier, Sieur de La Salle, named all of the land drained by the Mississippi River and its tributaries "Louisiana" in honor of Louis XIV, king of France.

Think about what other places are named after faraway places and people (examples: Plymouth, Massachusetts; Jamestown, Virginia).

▲ After the Revolutionary War, many battles were fought over land in the Northwest Territory.

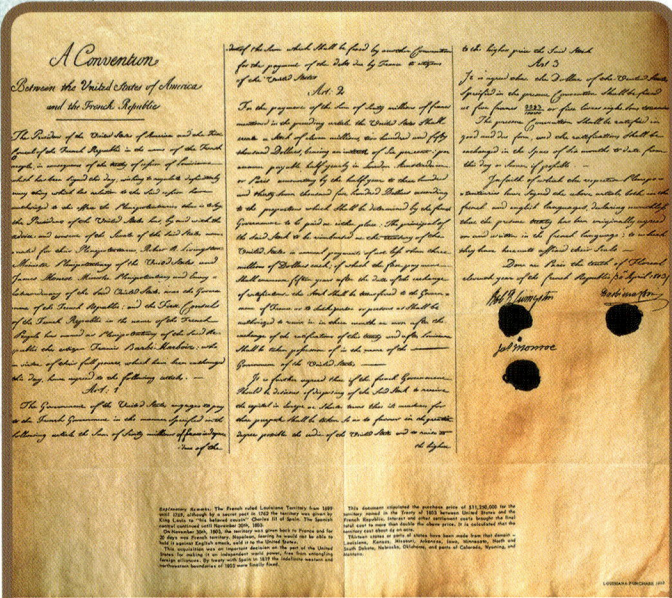

PRIMARY SOURCE

The Louisiana Purchase

The Louisiana Purchase has long been considered the greatest real estate deal in history and the most notable achievement of Thomas Jefferson's presidency. In 1803, the United States purchased approximately 2,145,000 square kilometers (828,000 square miles) from France for a sum of $15 million. (The United States paid France $11,250,000 and repaid debts owed to France by American citizens in the amount of $3,750,000 to square the deal.)

The acquisition of the Louisiana Territory for the bargain price of less than three cents per acre was lauded as a great victory for the young republic and its president. The ratification of the Louisiana Purchase treaty by the Senate on October 20, 1803, doubled the size of the United States and opened up the continent to its westward expansion. All told, fifteen states were eventually created—in whole or in part—from the land deal. You can read copies of the treaty at the Library of Congress or online at www.loc.gov.

The Louisiana Purchase

As the 1800s began, Emperor Napoleon Bonaparte of France was preparing for war against Great Britain—and in need of money. The third president of the United States, Thomas Jefferson, feared Napoleon would regain control of the strategic port of New Orleans from Spain and strangle the Mississippi trade routes relied upon by American settlers. He sent his foreign minister Jon Livingston and future president James Monroe to negotiate a deal, and they proved successful. France would agree to sell the land known as the Louisiana Territory to the United States for $15 million. The purchase doubled the size of the United States overnight.

▲ military general and first emperor of France, Napoleon Bonaparte

Summing Up

- American colonists were intrigued by the possibilities that might come from North American lands.

- The promise of being part of an entirely new nation drove early settlers to push into the wild, western interior of the North American continent.

TIME LINE

1763 King George III forbids American settlers from moving west beyond the Proclamation Line

1775 Daniel Boone opens the Wilderness Road into Kentucky

1785 The Ordinance of 1785 provides a system for selling government-owned lands in the Northwest Territory

1787 The Northwest Ordinance provides government for the Northwest Territory

1794 Native Americans are defeated in the Battle of Fallen Timbers, bringing peace to the Northwest Territory

1795 A treaty with Spain settles Georgia's border with Florida, which Spain continued to own

1803 The Louisiana Purchase opens a vast territory beyond the Mississippi River

PUTTING IT ALL TOGETHER

Choose one of the following research activities. Work independently, in pairs, or in small groups. Share your responses with your class, and listen to others present their work.

1 Write a paragraph in which you explain why many early Americans were so eager to see what was beyond the Appalachian Mountains. Include examples of what the settlers hoped to find.

2 With a partner, using the map on page 15, plan your trip west from one of the thirteen colonies. How far would you have to travel? What river(s) would you cross or travel on? You would be passing through lands controlled by different tribes of Native Americans. Which ones?

3 On page 15 you learned about the Ordinances (laws) of 1785 and 1787. Explain the purpose of each. Include examples of changes that came about as a result of the Ordinances.

BY WATER AND BY LAND

From 1763 to 1836, how did people travel and where did they go?

Americans on the Move

As of December 20, 1803, when the newly purchased Louisiana Territory became a U.S. possession, land-hungry Americans had hundreds of miles of new places to settle. At the dawn of the nineteenth century, water travel was the preferred method, especially for moving heavy things. Many wondered if there were rivers one might paddle all the way west to the Pacific. Eventually, people would create artificial waterways, called **canals**, on which they could float from one place to another. It was better than bumping along on America's roads. Most of them were little more than rocky, rutted trails.

Well into the 1800s, rivers were Americans' "roads," rippled by rafts, dugout canoes (like the Native Americans made), and canoes made of animal skin or tree bark. There were **flatboats** and **keelboats**, big boats that could be steered, paddled, and pushed with long poles against the stream's bottom, and later, steam-powered paddleboats.

Before Daniel Boone's family traveled from Kentucky to Missouri in 1799, Daniel spent months hollowing out a mighty poplar tree, turning it into a dugout canoe—18 meters (60 feet) long! In it would go most of his family and their belongings down the Ohio River to the Mississippi. Up on the riverbanks, sixty-four-year-old Daniel, his sons-in-law, and their packhorses and cattle all walked to Missouri.

▲ **The Louisiana Purchase (shaded) doubled the size of the United States.**

Americans came up with many ways to travel up and down their continent's river roads.

The Corps of Discovery

President Jefferson was a mentor to his private secretary, Meriwether Lewis. Working together, they designed an official military exploration into the unknown territory. As part of the plan, Lewis wrote to another Virginian, William Clark. As soldiers, they had both served under General Anthony Wayne, fighting the Native Americans of the Ohio Valley. Now these two young veterans would be **captains**, or leaders, of the Corps of Discovery, better known as the Lewis and Clark Expedition.

On May 14, 1804, after months of study and preparation, Captain Lewis, twenty-nine years old; his Newfoundland dog, Seaman; and Captain Clark, thirty-three, set out west from St. Louis on the Missouri River. One of their forty-four crew members was William Clark's slave, York, thirty-three, the only black explorer on the long mission, or **expedition**. Along with their 17-meter (55-feet) long keelboat, the crew paddled two smaller boats, called **pirogues**.

PRIMARY SOURCE
Diary of Lewis and Clark

Throughout the Lewis and Clark Expedition, the explorers kept detailed, often illustrated diaries. They recorded their progress, as well as almost 180 unfamiliar plants and 125 animals they saw, including lots of "barking squirrels" (now known as prairie dogs), according to Meriwether Lewis.

"I set out at 4 o'clock, P.M., in the presence of many of the neighboring inhabitants and proceeded under a gentle breeze up the Missouri to the upper point of the first island, 4 miles, and camped on the island."
—William Clark, May 14, 1804

After eighteen months, Clark thought he saw the Pacific Ocean at last. "Ocean in view! Oh! the joy," he wrote, on November 7, 1805. In fact, the explorers still had 32 kilometers (20 miles) to go. Clark had seen the bay at the mouth of the Columbia River.

Meriwether Lewis

William Clark

THEY MADE A DIFFERENCE

Sacajawea

Lewis and Clark's ambitious, dangerous undertaking took twenty-eight months. By boat, on foot, on horses, Captains Meriwether Lewis and William Clark had journeyed almost 12,900 kilometers (8,000 miles). They never would have made it without the help of Native Americans they met along the way, especially a young woman of the Shoshone tribe. Her name was Sacajawea.

▲ Sacajawea (right) was crucial to the success of the Corps of Discovery.

Lewis and Clark met Sacajawea and Toussaint Charbonneau, her fur trapper husband, at Fort Mandan, North Dakota, in late 1804. When the captains continued westward in the spring of 1805, Sacajawea and Charbonneau joined them. They served as guides, and as translators so the expedition could communicate with the Native Americans. Sacajawea traveled with her infant son strapped to her back. Clark believed that "a woman with a party of men is a token of peace."

The captains met nearly fifty tribes in all, presenting their leaders with peace medals stamped from a picture of President Jefferson. Only a small band of Blackfeet gave the explorers any trouble. Near present-day Missoula, Montana, in July 1806, they tried to steal the expedition's horses and guns. Two of the Native Americans were killed in the fight that broke out.

It is unclear what became of Sacajawea after she and her husband and son parted with the expedition on the return journey. But it is certain that the explorers made it back to St. Louis on September 23, 1806, thanks, in part, to Sacajawea.

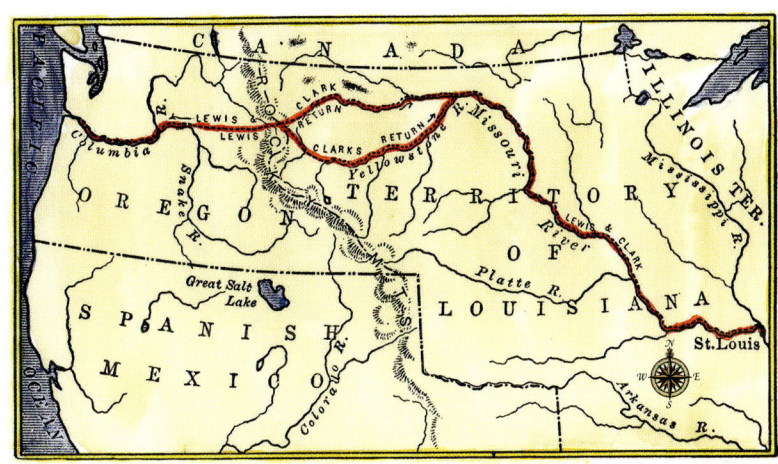

◄ Lewis and Clark's Corps of Discovery covered more than 12,900 kilometers (8,000 miles) during its 28-month expedition.

The Rocky Mountain Fur Trade

Lewis, Clark, and other explorers, such as Zebulon Pike, who led an official expedition into America's Southwest in 1806–1807, returned with extraordinary stories. Captain Pike and his men followed the Arkansas River into present-day Colorado, where they first sighted Pikes Peak, named after the expedition's leader. These rugged men told about the country's unexpected vastness, its beauty, and the great numbers of animals to be found. As Meriwether Lewis wrote in his journal (April 19, 1805, in present-day North Dakota): "The beaver of this part of the Missouri [River] are larger, fatter, more abundant and better clad with fur than those of any other part of the country. . . . Their fur is much darker." By 1807, Manuel Lisa, an ambitious Spanish merchant who had settled in St. Louis, was leading an expedition up to what is now Montana. Among the men were veterans of the Corps of Discovery. In 1809, the St. Louis Missouri Fur Company sent keelboats up the Missouri, loaded with men, who set up more fur forts, where traders swapped goods for pelts that were brought in by European and Native American trappers. In 1810, John Jacob Astor of New York founded the Pacific Fur Company. In 1811, he sent men to set up Astoria, a fur-trading post on the coast of Oregon. It became the first permanent settlement west of the Rocky Mountains.

The quest for fur caused conflict as the fur companies competed for control of different parts of western North America. Some tribes along the upper Missouri River, such as the Blackfeet and the fearsome Arikara, were so unhappy with fur traders and trappers that they attacked groups of them.

HISTORY & LITERATURE

James Beckwourth

James Beckwourth was an African American mountain man, fur trader, and explorer. He detailed his life history to Thomas D. Bonner, author of the book *The Life and Adventures of James P. Beckwourth: Mountaineer, Scout, Pioneer and Chief of the Crow Nation*. Here is an excerpt:

"An old warrior despises the sight of a trap; hunting buffalo, even, does not afford him excitement enough. Nothing but war or a horse-raid is a business worth their attending to . . ."

▲ James Beckwourth played an important role in the exploration and early settlement of the American West.

HISTORICAL PERSPECTIVE

The Mountain Men's Rendezvous

Fur traders William H. Ashley and Andrew Henry advertised for adventurous men to travel west across the prairies with wagons and pack mules. Then, they would fan out in small groups, setting their beaver traps in the Rocky Mountains' icy rivers and streams. After a year, the trappers and the company men would meet in a mountain meadow, where they bought and sold furs and enjoyed parties, games, and storytelling. The people showed off frontier skills, too, such as target shooting and tomahawk throwing. Their yearly trade fair was known as the "mountain men's rendezvous."

The first rendezvous was held near present-day Burntfork, Wyoming, in 1825. Over the next years, the trappers brought their fur harvests to other places in Wyoming and in Idaho and Utah. More and more European, African American, and Native American frontier folks and their families came to set up their tents around the carnival-like gatherings. Fur traders brought supplies and goods to sell from Missouri, at the western edge of the United States. Sometimes European visitors and American pioneers joined the fun.

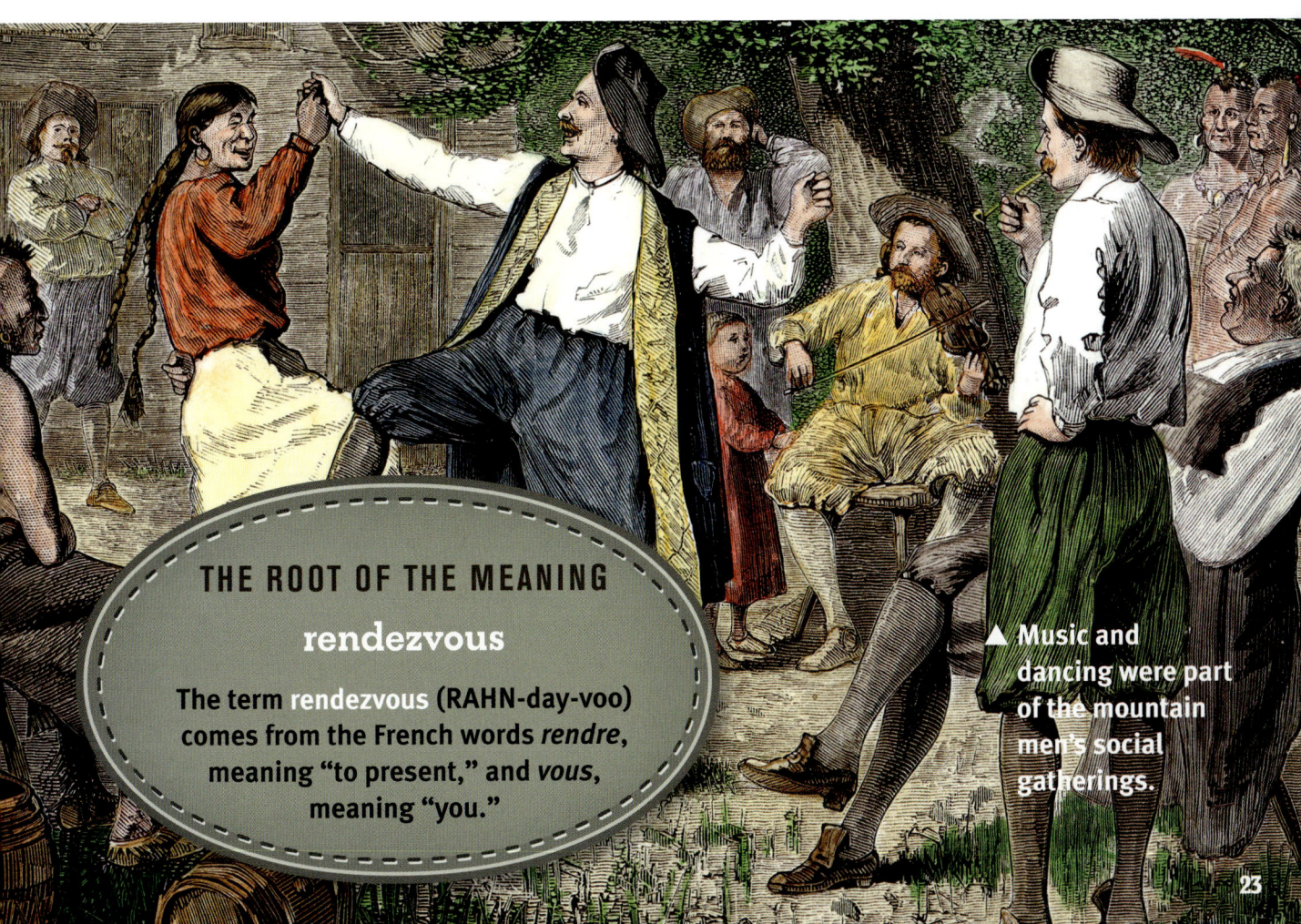

THE ROOT OF THE MEANING

rendezvous

The term rendezvous (RAHN-day-voo) comes from the French words *rendre*, meaning "to present," and *vous*, meaning "you."

▲ Music and dancing were part of the mountain men's social gatherings.

Improved Pathways

Mile by mile, early Americans worked to improve trails and rugged roadways, extending them ever westward. They also looked for the sturdiest wagons they could find. Some of the best had been made in Pennsylvania's Conestoga Valley since the early 1700s. These blue-painted **Conestoga wagons**, topped with European canvas covers, were made to ride high on their red wheels, to clear road rocks and tree stumps.

As early as 1806, the U.S. Congress voted for a government-funded east-west roadway. In 1811, strong workers with axes, picks, and shovels set to work in Cumberland, Maryland. The National Road, also known as the Cumberland Pike, would be built westward from there. By 1818, the road stretched 160 mountainous kilometers (100 miles) to present-day Wheeling, West Virginia. By the mid-1830s, the National Road was more than 965 kilometers (600 miles) long, ending in Vandalia, Illinois.

HISTORICAL PERSPECTIVE
The National Road

Today the United States is covered with a network of highways and lesser roads built with huge earthmovers and paved with asphalt. In fact, some of U.S. Highway 40 traces the path of the National Road. In early America, the work was done with axes, shovels, and other hand tools. Trees were chopped and sawed down; stumps and boulders were wrenched up and dragged away by strong people and animals. Hilly land was leveled and graded flat—all before the road could be surfaced.

Some roads were paved with wooden planks or thin logs, placed side by side across the path, then covered with sand. This was a bumpy "corduroy" road. But wood rotted quickly. The best, most laborious paving was found on a "macadam" road, named after John McAdam, the Scottish engineer who came up with the idea. This surface was made of layers of stones and gravel, broken with picks and heavy hammers. The 100-kilometer (62-mile) long Lancaster Turnpike, completed in 1794 in Pennsylvania, was paved that way. So was much of the National Road.

The Erie Canal

Six years after work began on the National Road, a crowd gathered in central New York on July 4, 1817. A groundbreaking celebration took place for the Erie Canal, which would extend from Albany to Buffalo in New York. An army of surveyors, engineers, craftsmen, and laborers worked on the great Erie Canal for eight years. It was 12 meters (40 feet) wide and 1.2 meters (4 feet) deep. Narrow boats, full of freight and passengers, would travel the waterway. A rope connected each boat to one or more horses or mules on the bank. As they walked, the boats moved along at a smooth 6 kilometers (4 miles) per hour.

▼ Mules and oxen strained to pull these heavy Conestoga wagons.

Because this water highway went up and down over hills, valleys, and rivers, the workers built eighty-three **locks**, or gates, and eighteen waterway-bridge combinations, known as **aqueducts**. When the Erie Canal was finished in October 1825, a farmer, merchant, or trapper from Ohio, for instance, could take his goods to Buffalo, New York. There, at the edge of Lake Erie, his cargo could be loaded onto a canal boat.

From Buffalo, the boats floated the 584 kilometers (363 miles) to Albany, New York. From there, people and cargo traveled down the Hudson River to New York City. The Great Lakes, America's inland, freshwater seas, were connected to the salty Atlantic Ocean and the rest of the world. Eastern and western Americans were connected, too. People and goods arriving at New York's harbor could cruise up the Hudson on a steamboat to the Erie Canal and on to the rest of America.

The Erie Canal had a major impact on both the cost of travel and the cost of transporting goods. It was a great opportunity for those who shipped their goods from their farms and factories in interior America to towns in the east. Before the great canal was built, it cost $41.25 to ship a ton of cargo from Buffalo to New York City. Afterward, the price fell to $4 per ton! This steep decrease in costs—and the huge increase in the amount of goods that could be shipped—were reflected in the prices and availability of consumer goods. Now western farmers and manufacturers could compete with their eastern counterparts.

HISTORY & LITERATURE

In his *American Notes for General Circulation*, English author Charles Dickens wrote about his 1842 ride on an American canal boat.

"I have mentioned . . . the sleeping arrangements. . . . I found suspended on either side of the cabin, three long tiers of hanging bookshelves, . . . on each shelf a sort of microscopic sheet and blanket; . . . As to the ladies, they were already abed, behind the red curtain, which was carefully drawn and pinned up the center. . . . Between five and six o'clock in the morning we got up, and some of us went on deck, to give them an opportunity of taking the shelves down; while others, the morning being very cold, crowded round the rusty stove, cherishing the newly kindled fire. . . . The washing accommodations were primitive. There was a tin ladle chained to the deck, with which every gentleman who thought it necessary to cleanse himself . . . fished the dirty water out of the canal, and poured it into a tin basin. . . . At eight o'clock, the shelves being taken down and put away and the tables joined together, everybody sat down to the tea, coffee, bread, butter, salmon, shad, liver, steak, potatoes, pickles, ham, chops, black-puddings, and sausages."

✔ CHECKPOINT
Talk It Over

As modern people, we use ever-changing technologies to satisfy our curiosity about the unknown and our need to get where we want to go quickly. How were Americans in the early nineteenth century the same? How were they different?

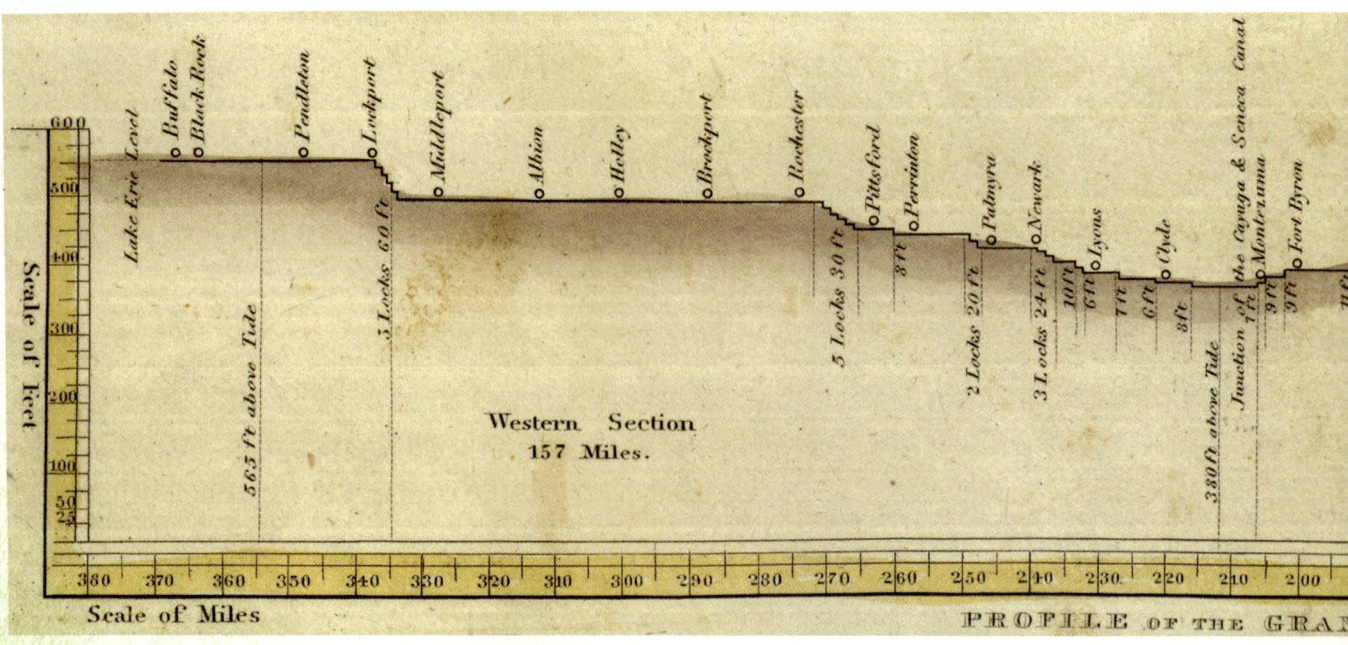

▲ The Erie Canal was the most successful human-built waterway in North America.

Into the South and West: The Santa Fe Trail

The Erie Canal was about half completed when trader and trapper William Becknell and four friends left Franklin, Missouri, on September 1, 1821, for points west. They had loaded packhorses and mules with cotton to sell in the old Spanish city of Santa Fe, in Mexico (present-day New Mexico). They sold it all not long after they arrived, on November 16, 1821. Over the next few years, thousands of people made the same 1,255-kilometer (780-mile) trip on the Santa Fe Trail, a new international trade route. Traders left with wagonloads of manufactured goods to sell and trade for burros, horses, furs, gold, and silver.

PRIMARY SOURCE

From one of William Becknell's letters, written to Bartolomé Baca on June 25, 1825:

"I traveled from the Spanish village of Taos, to Fort Osage, on the Missouri [River], in thirty-four days. I had supplied myself with provisions for the journey . . . meat, beans, & peas. By the route, which I traveled on my return, I avoided the so much dreaded sand hills, where adventurers have frequently been forced to drink the blood of their mules, to [quench] their thirst."

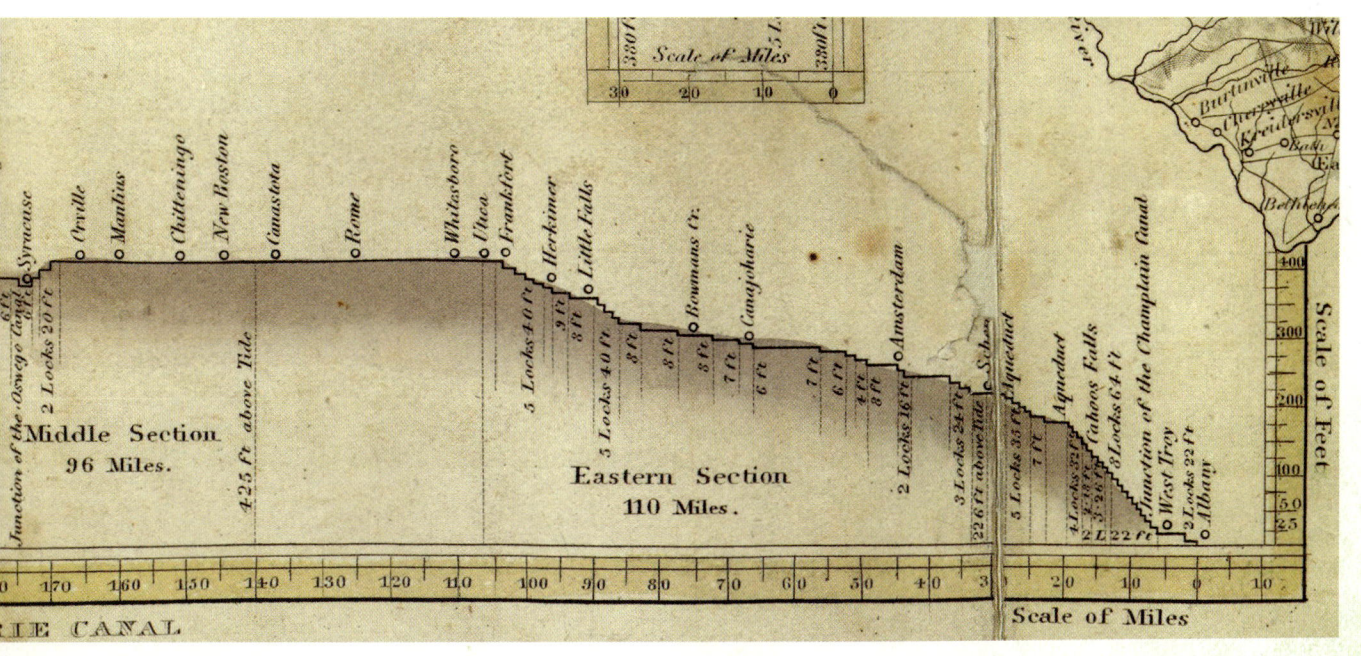

Most Americans in the early 1800s were neither trappers nor traders. They were land-hungry farmers, and the need for land grew along with the young nation's population. In 1821, Stephen F. Austin of Missouri led 300 settler families into Texas, then part of Mexico. Like nearly all of the countries of the Americas that had been part of the Spanish Empire, Mexico broke free in the early 1800s. And in 1819, Spain signed over its rights to Florida and southernmost Alabama and Mississippi to the United States. American pioneers poured into the area, upsetting and displacing the native people who had been living there for many generations.

In 1813, Creek Indians fought to defend their Alabama lands and their traditional way of life from European pioneers. By 1814, the Creek had lost the battle to an army led by future president Andrew Jackson. They were forced to sign away millions of acres of fertile lands in Alabama and Georgia. The next land war was with the Seminole of Florida, in 1817–1818. They were again overpowered by Jackson's army.

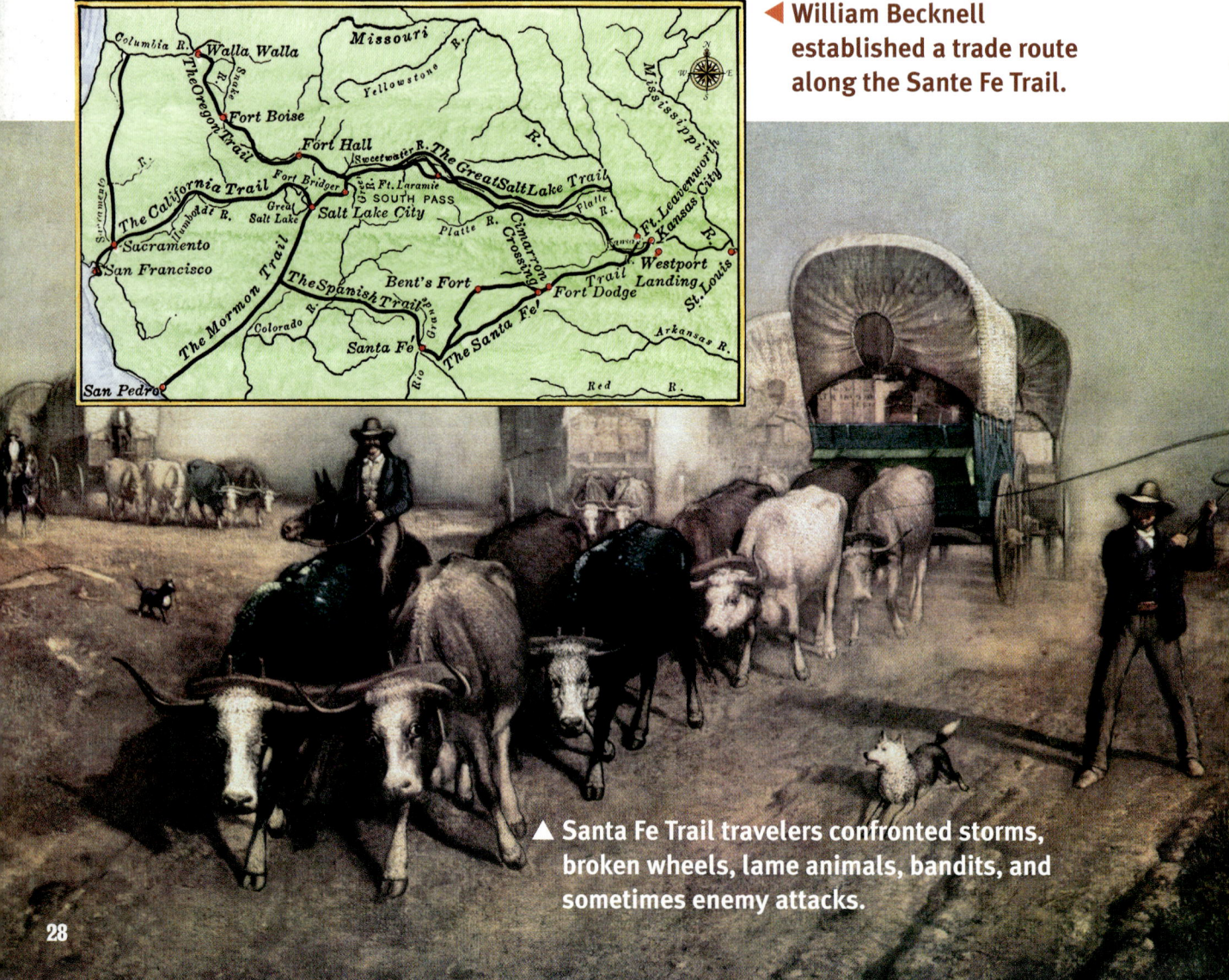

◀ **William Becknell established a trade route along the Sante Fe Trail.**

▲ **Santa Fe Trail travelers confronted storms, broken wheels, lame animals, bandits, and sometimes enemy attacks.**

Summing Up

TIME LINE

- In the early 1800s, the Louisiana Territory was explored and mapped by the Lewis and Clark and other expeditions.

- The National Road and the Erie Canal changed the way people traveled, and opened up opportunities for easterners and westerners.

- Spain ceded Florida, Texas, and part of Alabama to the United States. The Southwest opened up to explorers and settlers but only after violent battles with Native Americans living there.

1804 Lewis and Clark explore and map the northern Louisiana Territory

1811 The first steamboat travels the Mississippi River

1812 The War of 1812 against Great Britain begins

1813 Creek Indians fight to defend their lands in Alabama; they are defeated in 1814

1817 Work begins on the Erie Canal in Rome, New York

1819 Spain cedes (gives) Florida to the United States along with southern parts of Alabama and Mississippi

1821 Stephen F. Austin organizes an American colony in Mexican Texas; William Becknell opens the Santa Fe Trail

PUTTING IT ALL TOGETHER

Choose one of the following research activities. Work independently, in pairs, or in small groups. Share your responses with your class, and listen to others present their work.

1 On pages 20 through 22, you learned about the Lewis and Clark Expedition. Write a letter in which you apply to join the Corps of Discovery. Tell the captains why you wish to join their expedition, what and whom you hope to see, and how you plan to contribute to their explorations.

2 Investigate the remarkable generation of mountain men discussed on pages 22 and 23. Research their findings and some of their adventures. Present your findings in a written or oral report.

3 On pages 25 through 27, you read about the Erie Canal. In a couple of paragraphs, explain how you think it might have affected America's expansion.

A WARRIOR'S DILEMMA

CARTOONIST'S NOTEBOOK BY DENIS O'ROURKE AND SPENCER GONÇALVES ILLUSTRATED BY ALEX CAÑAS

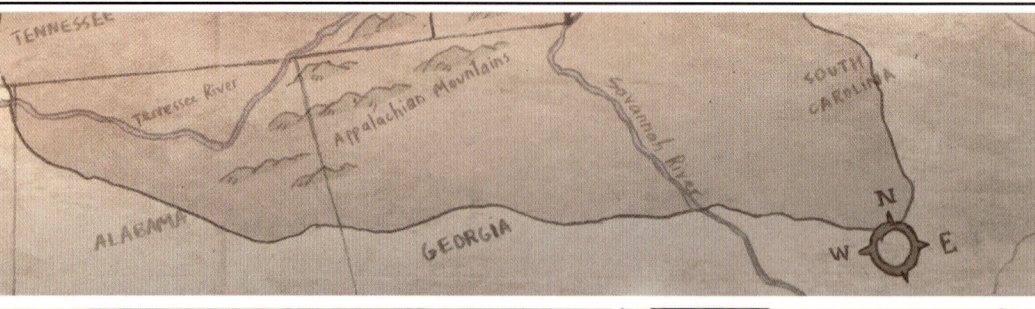

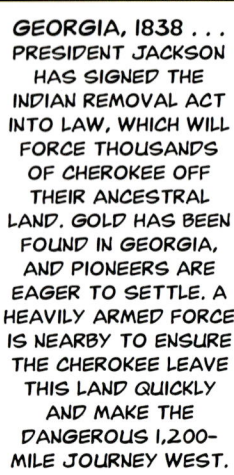

GEORGIA, 1838 . . . PRESIDENT JACKSON HAS SIGNED THE INDIAN REMOVAL ACT INTO LAW, WHICH WILL FORCE THOUSANDS OF CHEROKEE OFF THEIR ANCESTRAL LAND. GOLD HAS BEEN FOUND IN GEORGIA, AND PIONEERS ARE EAGER TO SETTLE. A HEAVILY ARMED FORCE IS NEARBY TO ENSURE THE CHEROKEE LEAVE THIS LAND QUICKLY AND MAKE THE DANGEROUS 1,200-MILE JOURNEY WEST.

WHAT IS IT?

ASHWIN!

THEY ARE CLOSE, ONLY A FEW DAYS AWAY! WE HAVE NOT THE SUPPLIES TO MAKE THIS LONG MARCH WITH THEM.

FOR GOLD AND COTTON, THEY WILL DRIVE US AWAY FROM THESE LANDS. . . I MUST THINK ON THIS.

SHOULD ASHWIN PLAN FOR THE WESTWARD JOURNEY, OR, SHOULD HE RESIST THE REMOVAL POLICY?

EXPLAIN YOUR ANSWER.

THE IMPACT OF A GROWING NATION

What were the consequences for Native American peoples as their traditional lands became U.S. territories and states?

Conflicts on the Frontier

Since the first Europeans settled on North America's eastern coast, there had been conflicts with the people who were already living there. In 1812–1815, the United States was again at war with Great Britain. British sea captains had been attacking U.S. ships on the Atlantic Ocean and forcing American seamen into the British navy. Great Britain hoped to regain control over America's Northwest Territory. Native Americans saw this War of 1812 as a chance to hold on to, or take back, their tribal lands from the United States. Along the wild frontier, from the Great Lakes, throughout the Ohio Valley, and down to Florida, if there was a pioneer settlement, Native Americans often attacked.

One Native American leader stood out from the rest. He was Tecumseh, a gifted speechmaker and respected leader of the Shawnee. Since early 1810, Tecumseh had been doing his best to accomplish what Pontiac had attempted in the 1760s: unite the Delaware, Miami, Winnebago, and other nations of the Ohio Valley so they could fight off the ongoing invasion by European settlers. Tecumseh's younger brother, Tenskwatawa, had a powerful spiritual message. "The Shawnee Prophet," as he was known, proclaimed that all of the Native Americans should return to their old ways and stand together. In that way, they would keep their tribal homelands and live happily on them.

▼ Besides traveling overland, many of the exiled Native Americans went west by way of the Tennessee, Ohio, Mississippi, and Arkansas Rivers.

PRIMARY SOURCE

Tecumseh

In 1800, the U.S. Congress had carved the Indiana Territory out of the older Northwest Territory. It included the future states of Indiana, Illinois, and Wisconsin, and parts of Minnesota and Michigan. At Vincennes, Indiana, on August 14, 1810, Tecumseh led a group of warriors to meet the governor of the Indiana Territory in a tense, but peaceful, confrontation. Here is a portion of Tecumseh's powerful statement to Indiana's territorial governor, William Henry Harrison.

"I am a Shawnee. My forefathers were warriors. Their son is a warrior. From them I take only my existence. From my tribe I take nothing. I am the maker of my own fortune. And oh, that I might make the fortune of my red people, and of my country, as great as the conceptions [ideas] of my mind, when I think of the Great Spirit that rules this universe. . . . Once they were a happy race. Now they are made miserable by the European people, who are never contented but are always encroaching [coming nearer]."

The settlers in Indiana Territory were increasingly nervous about the Native American presence. In late 1811, when Tecumseh was away, future president William Henry Harrison and about a thousand soldiers surrounded Prophet's Town. Just before dawn on November 7, Tenskwatawa and the Native American warriors attacked the troops, believing that their spiritual powers would protect them from the European men's bullets. Though they suffered heavy losses, Harrison's army won the resulting Battle of Tippecanoe and set fire to Prophet's Town. Most of the Prophet's followers left him. His reputation was ruined.

The United States declared war on Great Britain a few months later, in June 1812. Tecumseh led hundreds of Native American warriors, who fought alongside British soldiers against U.S. troops, in the harsh country around the Great Lakes. In a battle north of Lake Erie, Tecumseh was killed.

The Indian Removal Act

Tecumseh's younger brother, the Shawnee Prophet, died in eastern Kansas in 1836, the last year of President Andrew Jackson's administration. Long before his presidency, Jackson had commanded the U.S. troops who helped drive the Creek, Seminole, and other nations out of Georgia, Alabama, and Florida. During President Jackson's time in office, lawmakers **legislated** their most powerful act against Native Americans.

In 1829, the first year of Jackson's presidency, European settlers found gold on Georgia land belonging to the Cherokee people. In 1830, President Jackson pressed the U.S. Congress to pass the Indian Removal Act. The Cherokee, Creek, Choctaw, Chickasaw, and Seminole—all of the remaining Native American groups in the Southeast—had to sell their property and relocate to the brand-new Indian Territory, in present-day Oklahoma.

In May 1838, U.S. soldiers with weapons called **bayonets** rounded up Native Americans and began forcing more than 15,000 men, women, and children on a wrenching 1,600-kilometer (1,000-mile) journey. Some used boats, horses, or wagons, but most walked the whole way. Those who survived arrived in the Indian Territory in March 1839. More than 4,000 people became sick and died along the long, miserable journey known as the Trail of Tears.

Seminole and Creek Indians who refused to leave their lands followed a warrior named Osceola into Florida's Everglades. They disappeared into this vast, swampy forest and lived there, with the alligators, snakes, deer, pelicans—and hundreds of "Black Seminoles." These were both free blacks and runaway slaves, and their descendants.

✔
CHECKPOINT
Read More About It
Using your school library or online resources, learn more about the Cherokee and the Trail of Tears.

Beginning in 1835, Osceola and his warriors defeated U.S. troops in several small battles in the swamplands. The conflict became known as the Second Seminole War. Fires were set on sugar plantations, and homes and settlements were destroyed throughout the area. Osceola was captured in 1837 and died in 1838. The skirmishes continued even after thousands of Seminole were caught and forced to relocate in the West. By 1842, the Second Seminole War had ended. The U.S. government grew tired of spending millions to fight the last of the remaining Seminole. Their descendants continue to live in Florida.

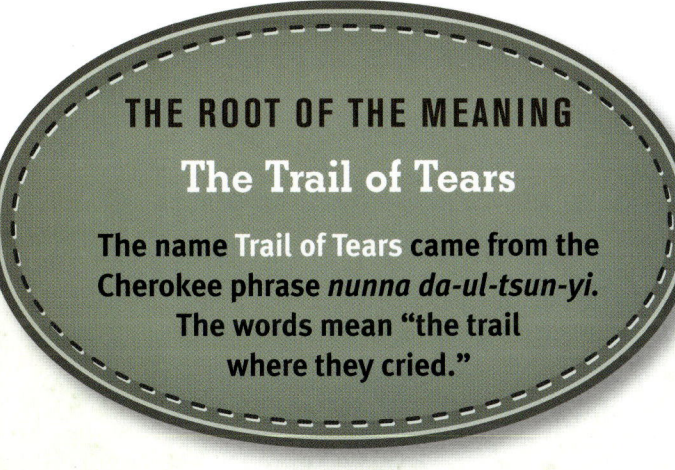

THE ROOT OF THE MEANING
The Trail of Tears
The name Trail of Tears came from the Cherokee phrase *nunna da-ul-tsun-yi.* The words mean "the trail where they cried."

◀ **An oil painting of Osceola by famous painter George Catlin**

The Black Hawk War

Native Americans in the north had been pushed west, too, but in the spring of 1832, an elderly warrior rebelled. According to an 1804 treaty, the Sauk (or Sac) and Fox tribes gave up their lands in Wisconsin and Illinois. Many of them had crossed the Mississippi River to live in Iowa, including sixty-five-year-old Black Hawk (Ma-ka-tai-me-she-kia-kiak) of the Sauk tribe. He believed the treaty was illegal and that the Native Americans had been tricked into signing it. In May 1832, Black Hawk and several hundred followers decided to return to Illinois and reclaim their village of Saukenuk (Rock Island, Illinois).

The European settlers who farmed and mined Illinois's valuable lead deposits were disturbed by the Native American presence. U.S. troops hurried to force the Native Americans out. The action became known as the Black Hawk War.

In June and July of 1832, many of the Native Americans fled back to Iowa. Others went north with Black Hawk into southern Wisconsin, where they clashed with U.S. troops. At last, in August, at the mouth of the little Bad Axe River, Black Hawk's band of 500 tired, hungry men, women, and children were trapped between U.S. soldiers on the east side of the Mississippi River and more soldiers aboard a riverboat.

The last fight of the Black Hawk War began on August 2 and is known by some as the Bad Axe Massacre. Black

▲ Black Hawk's "roach," or headdress, was made of stiffened, red-dyed deer hair.

Hawk himself described it months later in his autobiography, which he dictated to an interpreter. The Native Americans surrendered at Prairie du Chien, Wisconsin, on August 27, 1832.

"The **massacre** which terminated the war, lasted about two hours. Our loss in killed, was about sixty, besides a number that were drowned. The loss of the enemy could not be ascertained by my braves, exactly; but they think that they killed about sixteen, during the action."

Black Hawk was taken to American cities back east so people there could see the government's old prisoner. He died at age seventy-one, in 1838, on a reservation in Iowa.

Revolution in Texas

Since 1821, Americans led by Stephen F. Austin of Missouri had been resettling in the part of Mexico known as Texas. By the 1830s, some 25,000 American Texans lived there. The Mexican government grew uneasy with so many Americans living in its territory. After General Antonio Lopez de Santa Anna became **dictator**—completely controlling Mexico—in 1834, Texans knew they would have to organize. Texans declared their own revolutionary government in 1835 and took the city of San Antonio from Mexican forces. In the next year, a group of rebel Texans faced nearly 5,000 Mexican soldiers. Some 200 men, women, and children sought safety behind the thick walls of an old Roman Catholic mission, San Antonio de Valero. Locals called it the Alamo, after the Spanish word for cottonwood, a type of tree that grew in the region. Among the Texan rebels inside the Alamo were the young colonels William B. Travis, a former lawyer, and celebrated knife fighter James Bowie. Also there was Davy Crockett, age thirty-nine, a colorful Tennessee frontiersman and former U.S. congressman.

Colonel Travis sent out pleas for help to defend the small group against the overwhelming Mexican force, but few showed up. Inside the Alamo, all but two men fought for their cause. With cannon and rifles, the small band of Texans held off the Mexican army for thirteen days. Then, in the darkness before dawn on March 6, 1836, the Mexicans rushed over the battered walls of the mission. The Texans had little ammunition left. Most of them were sick and exhausted. The Mexican army shot or stabbed most of the people in the ferocious hand-to-hand battle. Any who survived were taken prisoner and later killed.

▲ Davy Crockett was often called "King of the Wild Frontier."

▲ Mexican general Antonio Lopez de Santa Anna proudly wore a Mexican military uniform.

PRIMARY SOURCE

On February 24, 1836, twenty-six-year-old Colonel William B. Travis wrote this letter from the Alamo:

"To the People of Texas & all Americans in the world — Fellow citizens & compatriots —

I am besieged by a thousand or more of the Mexicans under Santa Anna — I have sustained continual Bombardment & cannonade for 24 hours & have not lost a man —The enemy has demanded a surrender. . . . I have answered the demand with a cannon shot, & our flag still waves proudly from the walls —<u>I shall never surrender or retreat</u>. Then, I call on you in the name of Liberty, of patriotism, & of everything dear to the American character, to come to our aid. . . . The enemy is receiving reinforcements daily. . . . If this call is neglected, I am determined to sustain myself as long as possible & die like a soldier who never forgets what is due to his own honor & that of his country.

<u>Victory or Death</u>

William Barret Travis, Lt. Col. Comdt."

Death came to Colonel Travis less than two weeks later.

▲ Colonel William B. Travis of the Texas Army had been a lawyer in Alabama.

This might well have been the end of the Texan revolution, but U.S. general Sam Houston refused to declare defeat. In a surprise attack, U.S. forces defeated the Mexicans at the Battle of San Jacinto on April 21, 1836. Their battle cry, "Remember the Alamo," is remembered to this day. The day after the battle, Houston and his men captured General Santa Anna. The independent Republic of Texas was born.

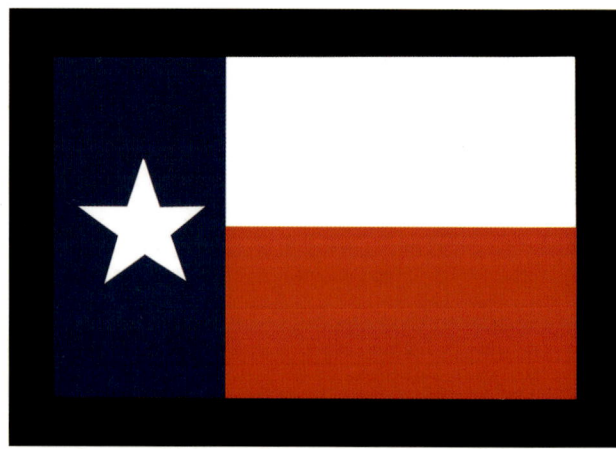

▲ The "Lone Star Flag" of Texas was formally adopted on January 25, 1839.

The Far Country

As war in Mexico raged, Dr. Marcus Whitman and his new wife, Narcissa, were making their way westward from New York. They traveled by stagecoaches, wagon trains, and steamboats. In Missouri, they planned to prepare for their overland journey to the faraway Oregon Country. In the 1830s, this region included much of present-day British Columbia as well as the modern states of Oregon, Washington, and Idaho, plus parts of Montana and Wyoming. At one time or another, parts of this beautiful region were claimed by Great Britain, Spain, the United States, and Russia because of the money to be made from fur. Multitudes of thick-coated beavers lived in and by the Oregon Country's rivers, lakes, and streams.

Only twenty-three years had passed since Americans had been forced to give up their trading post at Astoria during the War of 1812. In the 1830s, the man in charge of the region was John McLoughlin, an employee of Great Britain's powerful Hudson Bay Company, an important player in the international fur trade.

Dr. and Mrs. Whitman were not interested in participating in the fur trade, but they were interested in ministering to the many Native American tribes who lived in the Pacific Northwest. These included the Nez Percé, Blackfeet, Cayuse, Tillamook, and Yakima. The Whitmans and another couple on the wagon train, Henry and Eliza Spalding, were

▲ Marcus Whitman   ▲ Narcissa Whitman

▲ This image shows Narcissa Whitman caring for a sick Native American during one of the Whitmans' missionary expeditions.

Christian missionaries. They were passionately determined to share their faith with Native Americans. To be safe, they traveled part of the way from Missouri with fur traders. They stopped at the 1836 Mountain Man Rendezvous, too, beside Wyoming's Green River.

PRIMARY SOURCE

Narcissa Whitman's letter of June 3, 1836. Mountain man Thomas Fitzpatrick was the "captain," or leader, of her wagon train.

"The Fur Company is large this year; we are really a moving village — nearly 400 animals, with ours, mostly mules, and 70 men. The Fur Company have seven wagons drawn by six mules each, heavily loaded. . . . If you want to see the camp in motion, look away ahead and see first the pilot and the captain, [Thomas] Fitzpatrick, just before him, next the pack animals, all mules, loaded with great packs; soon after you will see the wagons, and in the rear, our company. We all cover quite a space. The pack mules always string one after the other just like Indians."

▼ **This painting is based on an 1846 sketch by Dr. Marcus Whitman, medical missionary.**

Today our cars easily travel 16 kilometers (10 miles) in ten minutes. Wagon trains then covered only 16–24 kilometers (10–15 miles) per day. Between May and September 1836, Narcissa Whitman and Eliza Spalding became the first American women to pass through the streams, rivers, prairies, and rugged Rocky Mountains of the West. They ventured all the way to the wild Columbia River and the Pacific Ocean on fur trappers' trails that, altogether, would become the great Oregon Trail.

The Whitmans established a mission near present-day Walla-Walla, Washington, but their story did not end happily. They were murdered in 1847 by their Cayuse neighbors, whose families were dying in a measles epidemic. European settlers swarming into their lands had likely brought the deadly viruses with them.

Summing Up

- Americans living in the mid-1800s might have been proud of their nation's growth since the United States won its independence in 1783. They also had good reason to question the cost of their country's expansion and progress.

- Loss of life due to violent conflict, backbreaking labor, and broken promises was the price paid by many Native Americans.

TIME LINE

1817 First Seminole War

1825 New York's Erie Canal is completed

1830 U.S. Congress passes the Indian Removal Act

1832 Black Hawk War

1835 Second Seminole War

1836 Fall of the Alamo; Texan independence

1836 Fur trappers lead missionaries west, including the first female U.S. citizens to travel overland to Oregon

1838 The Cherokee and other tribes begin journey along the Trail of Tears

PUTTING IT ALL TOGETHER

Choose one of the following research activities. Work independently, in pairs, or in small groups. Share your responses with your class, and listen to others present their work.

1 Reread this chapter and, with a partner, make a list of six of the real-life characters from this time period whom you would like to meet. Tell why you would like to meet each of them.

2 Using online resources in your school's library and what you learned on pages 32 through 35, research the Indian Territory. Write a few paragraphs about it, including what Native American tribes still live in modern-day Oklahoma.

3 Explain in a paragraph or two how the fur business affected the story of America.

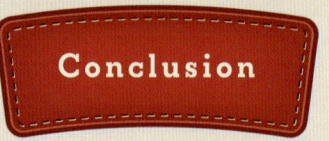
A NEW BEGINNING

In the decades before the Whitmans began their journey in 1836, countless people had gone westward. Each had his or her reason for going. They wanted furs and farmland. They wanted to get away from troubles back east. They wanted new opportunities out west. As pioneers and trappers kept moving on, deeper into North America's wilderness, surveyors came along to measure and map what seemed like a never-ending land. People came up with new and improved ways of traveling ever westward. And all along, the newcomers made and broke promises to those who had lived there first. To these Native Americans, the tide of European settlers seemed never-ending.

The story of America's westward expansion is one of heroic effort and technological achievement. The whole story can never be known; as with other chapters in United States history, so much lies unrecorded in the vanished past. But we do know, and should not forget, that in the case of the Native Americans, a great part of our nation's story is one of cultural misunderstandings, bigotry, deceit, and war.

In the thirty-three years between the Whitmans' 1836 adventure and the completion of the transcontinental railroad in 1869, more than 500,000 pioneers, plus countless horses, mules, and oxen, would leave western Missouri and travel the great overland trails to Oregon and California, nearly 3,200 kilometers (2,000 miles) away. Theirs was a powerful chapter in the long, remarkable, and complicated story of America's expansion into the West.

HOW TO WRITE A DIARY ENTRY

A diary or journal entry is a first-person account that describes and records an event. People keep diaries for many reasons. Some people record their hopes and dreams in a diary. Some use diaries to record their descriptions and feelings with regard to daily events or ongoing subjects. Often people want to keep a record of an important time or event, knowing that it will be useful in the future for others to understand. Diaries are a valuable primary resource that can tell us a lot about how people lived and what they thought in the past.

You can keep a diary in a notebook or on a computer.

1 Decide on a time and format to write an entry each day or each week—perhaps writing each morning in a notebook or each evening on the computer.

2 Begin your diary entry. Start with the date and day of the week (future readers will want to know).

3 Write using the first person. Use the pronoun "I."

4 Choose an experience that was important to you and describe the event or situation as well as your feelings about it. Be sure to include the following in your entry:

- Your location: What does it look like around you? What things and/or animals do you see?

- Who are your companions, if any?

- Where do you go? And how do you travel?

- What happens?

- How do you feel?

5 Reread your diary entry and revise if necessary.

For example, here is what Narcissa Whitman wrote in her journal, in what is now western Wyoming, on July 25, 1836:

"Came fifteen miles today; encamped on Smith's Creek, a small branch of Bear Creek. The ride has been very mountainous—paths winding on the sides of steep mountains. In some places the path is so narrow as scarcely to afford room for the animal to place his foot. One after another we pass along with cautious step. Passed a creek with a fine bunch of gooseberries, nearly ripe."

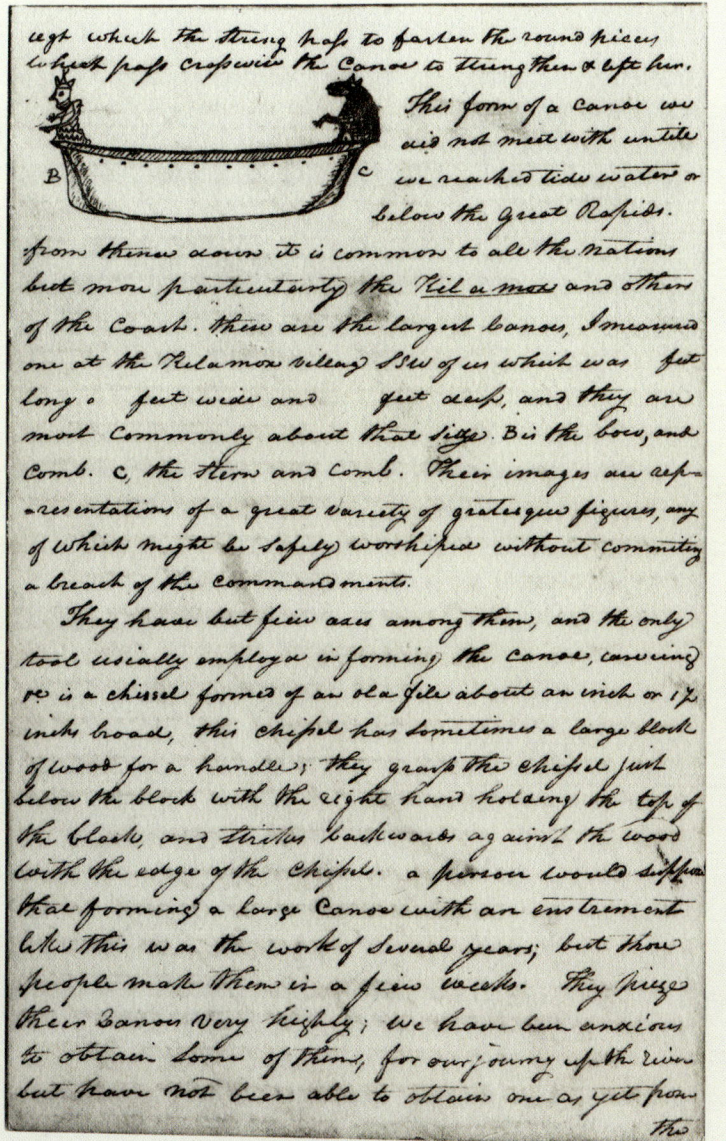

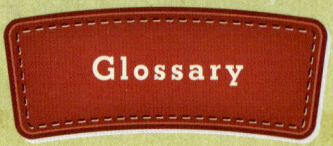

Glossary

aqueduct (A-kweh-dukt) *noun* a large structure that carries in water from faraway places (page 25)

bayonet (BAY-uh-net) *noun* a blade attached to the end of a rifle (page 35)

canal (kuh-NAL) *noun* a long, narrow, man-made waterway designed for boat travel or for watering land (page 18)

captain (KAP-tun) *noun* the person who acted as leader of an expedition or a wagon train (page 20)

Conestoga wagon (kah-neh-STOH-guh WA-gun) *noun* a heavy wagon (often painted blue), with big, broad wheels, originally built in Conestoga, Pennsylvania (page 24)

dictator (DIK-tay-ter) *noun* person who rules with unlimited power (page 37)

diplomatic (dih-pluh-MA-tik) *adjective* involving the work of maintaining good relations between governments of different countries (page 14)

expedition (ek-speh-DIH-shun) *noun* a long journey intended to achieve a particular goal or mission (page 20)

flatboat (FLAT-bote) *noun* a rectangular, flat-bottomed boat used in shallow water to move freight and steered with a long rudder (page 18)

keelboat	(KEEL-bote) *noun* a shallow boat used on the Mississippi and Missouri Rivers to carry freight (page 18)
legislate	(LEH-jis-late) *verb* to make laws (page 34)
lock	(LAHK) *noun* a gated section of a canal in which the water level can be raised or lowered (page 25)
massacre	(MA-sih-ker) *noun* the slaughter of a large number of people (page 36)
ordinance	(OR-dih-nents) *noun* a law or decree made by a government authority (page 15)
pelt	(PELT) *noun* the skin of an animal with the fur still on it (page 6)
pirogue	(PEE-roge) *noun* a boat shaped like a canoe but larger (page 20)
Proclamation Line	(prah-kluh-MAY-shun LINE) *noun* a law made by King George III created this imaginary line through the Appalachian Mountains; designed to keep European settlers out of Indian lands (page 12)
surveyor	(ser-VAY-er) *noun* a person who lays out boundaries or routes on land (page 8)
territory	(TAIR-ih-tor-ee) *noun* a region or part of a country under a government's control, but not organized as a state (page 12)

Index